Desperate Trust

Desperate Trust

Kimberly Allison

Copyright © 2016 Kimberly Allison
All rights reserved.

ISBN: 1533514070
ISBN 13: 9781533514073
Library of Congress Control Number: 2016918703
CreateSpace Independent Publishing Platform
North Charleston, South Carolina

All scripture quotations are taken from the King James Version of the Bible unless otherwise noted.

Scripture quotations designated MKJ are from the Modern King James version.

For scripture quotations marked GW:
Scripture is taken from GOD'S WORD®, © 1995 God's Word to the Nations. Used by permission of Baker Publishing Group.

For scripture quotations marked NET:
Scripture quoted by permission. Quotations designated (NET) are from the NET Bible® copyright ©1996-2016 by Biblical Studies Press, L.L.C.http://netbible.com All rights reserved.

For scripture quotations marked NKJV:
Scripture taken from the New King James Version®. Copyright © 1982 by Thomas Nelson. Used by permission. All rights reserved.

Scripture quotations marked HCSB are taken from the Holman Christian Standard Bible®, Copyright © 1999, 2000, 2002, 2003, 2009 by Holman Bible Publishers. Used by permission. Holman Christian Standard Bible®, Holman CSB®, and HCSB® are federally registered trademarks of Holman Bible Publishers.

For scripture quotations marked NASB:
"Scripture taken from the NEW AMERICAN STANDARD BIBLE®, Copyright © 1960,1962,1963,1968,1971,1972,1973,1975,1977,1995 by The Lockman Foundation. Used by permission."

Scripture quotations marked (NLT) are taken from the Holy Bible, New Living Translation, copyright © 1996, 2004, 2007 by Tyndale House Foundation. Used by permission of Tyndale House Publishers, Inc., Carol Stream, Illinois 60188. All rights reserved.

Table of Contents

1.	What Happened?	1
2.	Looking Back	3
3.	Baby Number One	5
4.	Baby Number Two	8
5.	Baby Number Three	10
6.	Baby Number Four	12
7.	Baby Number Five	14
8.	Baby Number Six	16
9.	Newby's Story	19
10.	Coach's Story	22
11.	Pop's Story	24
12.	Aftermath	27
13.	Encounter with God	30
14.	NICU Experience	33
15.	Homegoing	35
16.	Funeral	37
17.	Dreams	39
18.	Guilt	41
19.	Questions	43
20.	Decisions	45
21.	Heart Pain	47
22.	Comfort	49
23.	Another Baby?	51

24. Searching	53
25. Hidden Pain	55
26. How Big is God?	58
27. Ministry	60
28. Anniversary	62
29. Monument	64
30. The Test	67
31. Mysteries	69
32. The Announcement	71
33. Prayers	73
34. The Crash	75
35. Delivery	77
36. Mopping Up	80
37. Anger	83
38. Purpose	86
39. Surprises	88
40. New Faces	90
41. Labor Room Madness	92
Afterward	97
References	99

What Happened?

I KNOW WHERE I am, but I don't know why. It's ICU where tubes and wires connect people to beeping machines. Whatever the reason, I know I must hear from God. I ask a busy nurse for a Bible. "Bible...Bible?" Echoes of "Bible" encircle the halls. Six Bibles appear from six directions at the same time. Six colors and sizes, at the end of six arms. Everyone laughs.

"I'll take...the BLUE one (like the one from High School Graduation). All leave. I'm alone with God. Open the Book. Hungry for the Word. What does it say? God, speak to me! Black marks on white paper make no sense. I can't read it! I never needed glasses; I just can't read it. Brain battery too low? Close the Book. Close the eyes. Tell me, Lord. Tell me verses. Verses of hope, peace, anything!

"Lord, thou hast been our dwelling place in all generations. Before the mountains were brought forth, or ever thou hast formed the earth and the world, even from everlasting to everlasting, thou art God" (Ps 90:1-2).

"Thank you, God. I was sixteen when I memorized those verses. Those are good. Now, give me another one."

"Lord, thou hast been our dwelling place in all generations. Before the mountains were brought forth, or ever thou hast formed the earth and the world, even from everlasting to everlasting, thou art God."

"Yes, I hear you, God. What else?" Hundreds of scripture passages hibernate in the back of my memory, but only one speaks now. Over and over, the same words. LORD, what are You trying to tell me? Is that all I need to know?"

Nurses tell people I'm asleep. But I'm praying. "Lord, speak to me. Give me wisdom."

I'm not in a panic. I'm in a dream. Viewing someone else's reality. I study mental snap-shots of the time before now: people's backs as they leave my room, saying goodbye. I can't see them coming in; can't see their faces; can't remember their conversations. Whole visits vanish. Only trailing edges are left. I remember people leaving, saying goodbye.

I recall the back of a nurse's head. She pushes buttons with her back to me and says, "We're not supposed to get attached to our patients, but there's something special about you." She has long curly hair, but I can't see her face. I watch her leave. I don't know her name.

Is it the medication, or is my mind protecting me, revealing selected safe memories, while hiding the rest?

The last "real life" I can summon is eating burritos with the kids at home on "D-Day" –Due Day. Grandmother cooks, Midwife chats. I kick back in recliner. Grandmother takes all five kids home with her; Midwife and I wait for Baby. That's it. Until this dream-life in ICU. It's Sunday.

Looking Back

TRY TO REMEMBER. Back to Friday. After burritos, kids are gone, I should rest. I can't rest - too nervous. So I talk. The midwife is here, like usual, but this is not Old Trusty Midwife. This is a New Midwife, whom I have never met before. Trusty, in nursing school fifty miles away, won't come unless we need her. She sends her friend, Newby. Newby tries Midwife Tricks to start labor. We've never done this before, but Trusty says we should. Hubs says we should. It is the due date, after all, and there has been some bleeding. Let's get it over with, they say. Easy for them to say.

Something feels very wrong, but I shove uneasiness off my thoughts. Just the same old dread of the same old labor, I self-talk. Let's get it over with. It will be all over soon. Stay calm.

We wait for labor to start. Newby asks why I choose midwifery for birthing. I recount believing that midwives disappeared with the Pharaohs of Egypt until I stumble onto a pregnancy book with Baby Number One. The book describes natural childbirth options, including the ancient midwife. This new/old idea of a midwife intrigues me. "Midwife" means "with woman." A female? I like that! A few phone calls and I find a small midwifery clinic tucked into a hospital one hour away from home. That's how it all starts.

We attend Lamaze classes and become armed with an array of pain distracting techniques. We plan on smiling all the way through the birthing experience while addressing announcements of the blessed event.

But the first birth is not the Sunday picnic we had planned!

I entertain Newby with bumbling delivery-room antics. She laughs; friendly lady.

Baby Number One

THE LAMAZE TEACHER said Breathe *Loud* and *Deep* when "game on." Your Partner will see, and hear, and spring into action. At 2:30 a.m., I run fast around our dining room table in circles, puffing and panting, propelled by pain. Steam locomotive on a downhill run, whistle blowing, and bell ringing.

Hubs stares at wristwatch through blurry eyes, rubs clammy hand over non-responsive face. He mumbles, "Tell me when one starts, so I can time it."

All hope of help from the Hubs disappears.

No need for goodie bag of suckers and tennis balls. Jump in the car for a one hour scream to the hospital. Hubs fears for his life, head whipping back and forth from highway to Crazy Lady in front seat of the car. His eyes are huge with terror, white showing all around the brown, mouth open with no sound. "Who is this woman!? Where did she come from!? What does she want from me?!"

My thrashing fingernails dig deep into Hubs' arm. He yelps, winces, searches for an escape. I'm on the bench seat with all fours, shouting in his ear. "Drive Faster! Run the red lights!" He punches the pedal with no regard. To anything. Blindly careening through intersections. Game on!

"Stop the car!" I need a ladies room.

An object in motion tends to remain in motion unless clawed and yanked by an unbalanced force. Car veers off to Denny's. Crazy Lady jumps out with car rolling. Must make it to the restroom. But not till pain ebbs. Speed walk around outside of restaurant, puffing and panting. Rub sides of belly with fingertips in big circles. Effleurage. Lamaze rule book says it might help. Sprint back and forth past full-length windows. Curious night owls gawk over coffee mugs. Big circles. Puff. Pant. Blow. Count. Full steam ahead! Pain won't stop. Run back to car, scramble in. No time for a ladies room.

Contractions don't wax and wane, like Lamaze Lady promised. It is one long hard squeeze, threatening to pop my body and kill me. "Hurry! Drive faster!" Gotta run. Gotta move. Pain will catch me if we slow down! No place to hide! Donkey kick Hubs as I spin around. Grab a handful of hair on the next gyration. "Hurry!"

The Hubs is bloody and bruised when we skid into hospital parking lot.

"Wait," he says. "Lamaze Rule Book says walk around the parking lot in case contractions stop in an unfamiliar setting."

I WANT contractions to stop. Hubs can walk all he wants. I'm running in.

Midwife declares, "You'll have this baby in thirty minutes!" I might live. Maybe.

Only one half of cervix is dilated. Midwife tries to manually make it happen. Yeow! Lamaze never saw this coming! Screaming, kicking, clawing, pushing hours go by; no baby.

Baby won't budge. Hubs stays in the corner of the room gaping, horrified. Watching the big game breathless. Long distance. Safe. Poor Grandmother gets all the bruises here.

Doctor comes in, eating a sub sandwich.

"Let's have a Look-See."

Look-See means *Reach-Feel*. Way up. All around.

"No cord around the neck. Hmmm."

Oxygen dropping, a line is drawn, "Baby within five minutes or we start cutting."

Mom up on haunches; crayon-blue First-born finally flops out with a whimper. We all whimper. First-born goes to ICU. I get stitches. Not the fairy-tale-all-natural birthing experience I had imagined. I'm mad. This is not in the Lamaze Rule Book.

What was the problem?

"Short cord," they say. "Tethered baby. It's a fluke. Never happen again."

It better not happen again!

But it does.

Baby Number Two

With First-born's horrific birthing experience still fresh on our minds, I do some reading. I research standard hospital birthing procedures and medications. My conclusion: altogether bad; totally unnecessary. I hard-sell Hubs on the idea of homebirth. I tell Hubs the human race survives thousands of years without hospital births. The female body is designed to give birth naturally. I report to him all the strange bacteria present in a hospital that are not in our home. I point to our mama cat, which hides under the porch to give birth; quiet, private. No one helps her. And everyone knows how intelligent cats are. I finally play my ace and tell him homebirth gives me the *home-team advantage*, and the former football player is sold.

Hubs agrees to let me try homebirth with Trusty Midwife for our next pregnancy. Trusty has delivered hundreds of babies and comes highly recommended.

Second pregnancy, Hubs and I analyze the game. I make a play book. "When I say *this*, you say *this*. When we get to *this* point, you do *this*." I write it down. He studies the plays. We review. On game day, he's ready. *Hubs* becomes *Coach*.

Trusty arrives at our home during the night, when babies usually make their appearance. This time, she brings a neo-natal nurse. Trusty always brings a different helper. She says she doesn't deliver babies; she catches them.

Coach is IN my face, eyes wide, white all around the brown, giving strong football pep talk, "Keep your eyes open! Blow! 1 – 2 – 3 – 4! Look at me! You can do it! Breathe in, breathe out! Eyes on the goal!" He laughs in my face to cheer me up. Coach never slacks. We pray, we cry, not pretty. No videos of the birth for me, thanks.

Thanks to Olympic-style body contortions, Second-born Beauty finally emerges crayon-purple. Another short cord. Coach snores loudly after the big game. I stare at the ceiling. I can't believe I chose another birth without pain medications. *What was I thinking? How many more will there be?* Keep repeating questions to self in the dark, amid hourly wobbles to bathroom.

Baby Number Three

W̱e'll get this figured out! Next time will be better! But third pregnancy we prop up painful varicose veins. Coach doesn't like that.

And third delivery has plateau of labor. No coach needed - nothing happening. Trusty Midwife ponders, "What were you doing when labor started?"

"Washing dishes."

"Go back to washing dishes."

It works. Contractions return with pots and pans. We make adjustment for short cord with birthing chair and gravity. Why didn't we do this before?! Long hours later, Lanky One screams out he's here. Coach even impresses his mother-in-law with his game-time finesse. He knows the playbook.

But a little further down the road, Coach realizes we're outnumbered. He starts to lose sight of the goal. "Maybe three kids are enough," he says. "Maybe this is all we can handle. Maybe we're finished..."

Oh, no! He's fading! Pray hard! *"Lord, we gave our family size to you! Coach is bailing out! Help!"*

I pray three days, *non-stop*, for coach to pick up the ball.

Day three: Coach sits at the dining room table, quietly thinking. He shares the story of an older lady he meets at work. She asks him, "Do you love children?"

Coach says, "Sure, I do."

She tells of growing up with seven girls, seven boys, all loving each other. All fun. She tells of her father's faith and musical abilities. He teaches each of the children to play instruments. They grow up loving, singing, and playing. She wouldn't have had it any other way. Then, later, all siblings play and sing together around their father's death-bed while he joins in, one last time. Beautiful. Sniff!

"So," Coach slowly, carefully concedes, "You can have as many kids as you want. And you need to take them to music lessons."

Coach is back in the game! And we get instruments to boot! Thank God for old ladies with stories!

Baby Number Four

EXCLUSIVE BREASTFEEDING WITH all our babies allows eleven to fourteen months of infertility for us. Heavenly spacing! We love babies, don't get me wrong! The Bible says babies are a blessing (Ps 127:3), and we don't reject blessings; but it takes a few years to forget the horrors of the previous birth. If only babies could arrive some other way! We relish some breathing room between pregnancies, so we are grateful for the two year spacing that comes from breastfeeding.

But the milk dries up when Lanky One is six months old. Oh dear! No natural contraceptive! Does God see this? Hello? We continue with normal married life, waiting for the ambush of a fertile egg. But God, who indeed sees this, delays conception for another thirteen months. Fourth birth will be almost two and a half years after third one. God truly does open and close the womb. He is bigger than all other circumstances. We are in good hands.

When fourth pregnancy gets underway, we get serious. We are fed up with short cords. Coach grills Trusty Midwife, "How long should the ideal umbilical cord be?"

"Twice as long as the baby."

Okay. We have a target. We pray for nine months for a cord twice as long as the baby.

Desperate Trust

Labor starts at a homeschool spelling bee. Midwife is called; family exits carefully, on tip-toe, and prepares to "man battle stations."

By now, we are pros at birthing. A Pro Team. I even add "Make orange juice" to the play book. Babysitters know their jobs and whisk little ones away before Mom gets loud. Don't want to scare the "littles."

But Fourth-Born Stocky One is big. And stuck. What's the problem? We prayed for a long cord! Trusty has a *Look-See.* That long cord is wrapped around Stocky One's neck. Trusty does a quick flip with skilled fingers, and baby is free.

I turn to Coach and snarl, "That HURT!"

I'm mad.

Coach doesn't get it. Of course, it hurt. Doesn't it always? Coach doesn't know my secret hope and belief that each successive baby will arrive with an easier birth. Who starts these nasty rumors?!

Baby Number Five

FIFTH PREGNANCY, WE huddle for a time out. Should we pray for a long cord? That didn't turn out so great. Short cord? No way. We decide to pray for God's will. Sure. That is what we want. God's will.

Family "counselors" and self-proclaimed prophets all speak as one unit to tell us we should be finished. "Five is enough," they say. "What if something should happen to 'the mama'?"

How silly! Something could happen to "the mama" even if I don't have any more children! I could have a wreck, cancer, accident! How ridiculous! We can't stop living just because something might happen!

Coach listens to advisors and prophets of doom. This will be our last one. But how will we stop the parade of babies? We agreed, when marriage was new, to let God choose our family size. We ceremonially flushed the pills down the toilet. No peace about contraception. All bad. We'll think of something later. After baby number five is born.

Good Friend reveals secret for contraction survival: with each contraction, bathe another child in prayer. Each contraction, pray for another 8 X 10 face on the mantle. Contractions peak, and I pray faster. Every future event in each child's life gets prayed for. Pain subsides. I'm in control. Four beautiful

8 x 10's, four contractions down. Out of kids, I start praying for neighbors. Then back through the 8 X 10's. When pain freaks out, I self-talk, "I can do this One More Time. This is our Last One."

Coach says, "This is the Last One." Trusty doesn't believe us.

Puff. Blow. This is the Last One. I can make it. The usual trip To Hell and Back, but less hysteria. This is the Last Time.

Pinky Dinky Fifth-Born arrives quiet and content, but she won't wake up to eat. Sleeps too much. I can't keep her awake at the breast. Doctor's X-ray shows broken clavicle. "Was she born faster than your other children?"

Who knows? I was praying for neighbors.

We survive. Pinky Dinky grows. This is our last one. What do we do now? We don't have to decide, yet. We can wait till I'm back to *normal*. Back to ovulating. We hold our breath for a year; still not back to *normal*. I always believe I will surely have thirteen children, but Coach feels the pressure to "do something about it." Pressure from everywhere.

Baby Number Six

BUT WHAT'S THIS? Signs of a pregnancy without starting back on a monthly cycle? Sixth pregnancy sneaks under the radar screen. Someone knows that Baby Number Six must begin the race of life without waiting for the starting gun. I guess we're not finished, after all! We laugh.

There is no good due date for Baby Number Six, so we have our first ultrasound. Ever. Don't tell me if it's a girl or boy. I want a surprise. Baby due in September. Just like I thought. Mamas know these things.

Advisors and prophets shake their heads and ask one another, "Don't they know what's causing this?"

They don't understand. They can't imagine why anyone would *want* more than one boy and one girl. "What will you do with them, anyway? How much will they cost?"

They don't see the heart. What if, by refusing more children, we inadvertently reject the future chemist who will solve the mystery of cancer? What if we say "No" to conceiving the leader of a great spiritual awakening in America? Even a "defective" child can encourage others to pursue their full potential in life. Every child has a purpose, determined before the earth was created (Eph 1:4). We don't worry about money because God pays for what He orders.

But most of all, I enjoy the Big Family. I love the hub-bub, the fun. In the living room we run laps around the sofa for P.E. We learn Bible verses with squeaky animal voices, earning a cookie for getting it right. We home-school and home-play. Out to eat, dress alike, we rehearse rules in the parking lot: Don't crawl under the table. Don't wipe messy hands on your clothes. Talk softly. Smile. People are watching. People always watch.

One wrinkled lady passes wrinkled dollars to matching brood of children. I'm proud. Proud of my Belly showing one more on the way. Smiling proud Mother of a matching flock.

But for the first time, I'm worried.

"Aren't you afraid to have your babies at home?" They always want to know. Strangers, friends, family ask every time.

Every time, I answer, "If I were afraid, I wouldn't do it." Every time, I have a greater fear of the hospital than of a home-birth. Every time, I assure myself that if I ever *do* feel afraid, I will choose a different course. But this time, with Baby Number Six, I'm nervous.

I know homebirths are for low-risk pregnancies, and I am anything *but* low-risk. I ask Coach. He says to ask Trusty. She says my risk factors are the same as always. She is not concerned. Coach is not concerned. Why am I concerned?

Am I caving in to fears from the enemy? I pray. A LOT. I weigh pros and cons. Coach growls if I ask him the same question twice, so I ask God over and over, "What should I do?"

One intense prayer, I glance two ambulances for two people and feel one of us won't make it. Just a glimpse in the corner of my thoughts. Where did that come from? Too fleeting to be a vision, surely. Is it from the Lord or the enemy? Is it a "knowing" or stray daydream? Don't give way to fear.

I pray while I cook, clean, fold. I pray without ceasing. Making the bed, I recall a passage from a children's book about Hudson Taylor (Thompson, p. 110). Missionary to China, he agonized over a decision that might involve danger and death, for himself and others. The thought that freed him: If God was urging him to do it, then all the responsibility for what happened would be God's, not his!

A measure of peace, and now, steady on course. Keep the game plan. Homebirth.

Years of hindsight and study later, I nod teary-eyed. God's path sometimes winds through the valley of the Shadow of Death.

Shadows.

Death.

Following Jesus doesn't mean easy. The narrow way is strait - *difficult*. But in the Shadow of Death, I will fear no evil (Ps 23:4). God is responsible for where He leads me. He's the shepherd. I'm the sheep.

But what happened? I remember Friday burritos and talking with Newby; then the brain skips to Sunday in ICU. Will someone fill me in? Later, I ask three people, Newby, Coach, and Pops, to tell me everything they remember.

Newby's Story

TRUSTY MIDWIFE CALLS to check on progress of labor with Baby Number Six. Contractions are mild. Not much happening. Trusty says she will come down later, if Newby wants to go home. Newby hangs around a little longer. Good thing.

Baby slams down hard. Dizzy. Pain. Sick. Little Mama panics, "Am I going to die?"

Newby says, "No – breathe deep. Slow, calm. Trusty is on her way." Newby thinks Little Mama is overreacting to pain. She doesn't know that something is terribly wrong.

"Call Grandmother – Don't bring the kids back yet. Call Coach – come home, now!" Newby goes out to her car to get birthing stool and … oxygen … just in case. Good thing.

Newby sets up birthing stool. Little Mama collapses. Newby calls Little Mama's name, checks pulse, sees blue fingernails and lips, tonic limbs. Starts CPR. Seizures begin. Newby calls 911 on the house phone - no response. Dials "O" - no response. Gets Trusty's cell number from coloring book by the phone where she had jotted it down earlier. Good thing. Trusty, on the highway, pulls over to call Grandmother, "Call an ambulance!" Grandmother thinks Trusty is calling an ambulance, and drives to Little Mama's house. She sees Newby doing CPR.

"What happened?!"

"Did you call an ambulance?"

"No, I thought one was already called!"

No reading glasses, can't read numbers in the phone book, Grandmother calls every number she knows by heart, but no one answers. Grandmother jumps in her car and races to Aunt's house. "Someone call an ambulance!" Grandmother speeds back with Aunt. They pray loud and hard, while Newby performs CPR.

No one hears the pounding on the door. Front door always sticks - can't be opened from the outside. Two ambulances drive away slow; they write in log "denied entrance."

CPR brings no response. Newby periodically checks for a heartbeat with Doppler. None.

Blood runs from Little Mama's mouth. Teeth are clenched.

"Where is the ambulance?!" All wonder. More CPR.

Coach arrives on the scene, ready for the "Big Game." Confusion everywhere. Women praying, Loud. Coach finds blue wife, fetal position, not breathing. Newby shouts orders: "Hold her legs up in shock position! Talk to her!"

Coach plays the role he knows best. "Hang in there! You can do it! Just a little bit longer!"

Newby detects Little Mama's heartbeat! Thank God! Keep doing CPR breathing, suction blood from mouth with bulb syringe, administer oxygen.

Little Mama starts moaning, flailing, kicking. Baby coming.

Meanwhile, two ambulance drivers sit in church parking lot to study options. Preacher-Cop comes out to offer help and hears their story. He tells them, "I know the family. I can get you in. Follow me."

Forty-five minutes from ambulance phone call, Preacher-Cop kicks the door open. Paramedics and sheriff deputies burst into the house as Baby Number Six makes his appearance.

Newby shouts orders: "This mom needs oxygen! Get a line going! Treat for shock!"

Now, the hemorrhaging starts. All see. "Rush to the hospital!" Paramedics load two people into two ambulances. Coach knows the play book like the back of his hand: If Little Mama and Baby are ever separated, go with Baby. Protect Baby. Little Mama always insists she can take care of herself, so Coach rides in ambulance with Baby.

Newby runs back into the house. Blood on her face, hair a mess; she grabs a clean shirt from Little Mama's closet. Paramedic comes in to get Newby. "I need you to ride with us. I need your help."

Newby rides with Little Mama to hospital. Driver phones ahead. Newby hears Little Mama mumbling, "Where am I? Where are we going? Why?"

"You had a beautiful baby boy."

"Who did? *I* did? Where am I?"

Newby hopes Little Mama will be OK - no oxygen for so long. She listens close to hear mumblings under oxygen mask: "Jesus." She prays with Little Mama.

Finally at the hospital, Newby sighs, relieved. Everything will be all right, now. Surely.

Coach's Story

COACH CHARGES INTO ER with paramedics. Nurses try to stop him. "Sir! You can't go back there!"

"You'll have to get someone bigger than me to make me leave." They can't find anyone bigger, so they let Coach stay. He stands out of the way of fast-moving ER staff, by the wall between Wife and Baby Boy. Coach answers questions about age, blood type, number of children, while blood pours off gurney. Both arms have I.V. blood lines. Towels coming. Blood pouring in; blood pouring out.

Wife asks Coach a quiet question. "Am I going to die?"

"No!"

"Then why did you bring me here?! You know I hate hospitals! Where's my baby?!" No blood in her ghost-white body, but her mouth still works. Loud.

Life-flight will take Baby Boy to NICU in Big City, fifty miles away. Helicopter Pilot snaps picture of Baby Boy before take-off. Coach goes with him. Pilot assures Coach it's a good place. Pilot says his baby was here, this same NICU. He says Baby Boy is in good hands.

After landing, scrub suits whisk Baby Boy away in a blur. Coach paces waiting room, praying for hope. Neo-Natal Doctor finds Coach, blurts: "Brain tests are showing no response. We'll do more tests, but I don't think he's going to make it."

Coach steels himself, steady. Then, a phone call from hometown friend: "You need to come back. ER Doctor says he doesn't think Little Mama is going to make it."

Coach's knees buckle. Mind reels. Where should he go? Where *does* he go? Knees bowing, he goes to God. "Lord, let them both live!"

Pop's Story

GRANDPARENTS ARRIVE AT ER. Coach and Baby Boy are gone to Big City NICU. Nurse comes out to waiting room and says, "Your daughter is a believer. Are you?"

"Yes."

"Then, PRAY. Get everyone you know to PRAY. It is very serious."

Pops goes outside to call church prayer chain. Grandmother (long ago nurse) asks who the OB Doctor is. He's a good one. "What's the problem?"

"They can't get the bleeding to stop. You can't go see her."

Pops is back. "We have to see her! Don't let her die by herself!" Finally, reluctant receptionist lets them through the door.

Grandparents don't recognize their daughter. White, swollen, screaming. Can't be her. OB Doctor steps back to let them pray. Talking and praying seem futile; Daughter does not respond, will not stop screaming. Grandparents hunker back to waiting room to be out of the way.

Later, Grandparents come back again. Daughter is alert and shivering, saying, "I am going to die. The pain is too much."

"No, you're not! You've got to fight this! You have kids to raise!"

"*You* raise the kids."

Pops gives a beautiful farewell speech that Daughter will never remember.

OB Doctor says, "I don't know what to do, don't know where to send her. Could do a hysterectomy, but it might make things worse; more bleeding…"

OB decides to prep for surgery, just in case. All friends and family hold hands in waiting-room, pray hard as Daughter is wheeled away.

Rolling down hallway, bleeding stops, tongue turns pink again. In operating room, OB decides against surgery. He'll keep everything intact.

Anxious friends in waiting room watch and pray. All look up to see Daughter rolling back past the windows, waving like a parade float. One friend quips, "I've been part of a Real Life Miracle!"

Daughter keeps saying "I can't breathe!" so OB places her on a ventilator. She really means it *hurts* to breathe because of cracked ribs from CPR, and now it hurts more.

In recovery room, Grandparents again don't recognize Daughter. Swollen and Fearful. Ventilator won't pump when she wants air. Nurses keep saying *Relax*. But Daughter panics and fights tubes, struggling to breathe. She grabs a nurse's clipboard and scribbles her only hope: "Pray!"

Pops prays, and Daughter goes to sleep. Nurses wake her up to check vitals. Panic starts again. Daughter pounds "Pray!" on clip-board. Pops prays, and she falls asleep again. Nurses are back. Panic is back. Protective Pops is ready to fight dutiful, unsuspecting nurses.

With her clip-board, Daughter commands every visitor to remove her from the suffocating ventilator. She can't breathe, and no one will help. Nurse finally takes the clipboard, and Pops kicks himself for not keeping the scribbled SOS notes.

Aftermath

ER DOCTOR AND OB Doctor sit at bedside in ICU. "Are we glad to see you! We didn't think you would make it!" they say.

What do they mean? I feel just fine (with morphine!). Painful smile with cracked lips. "Thank you." I have no idea what they are talking about. Just smile and nod.

Later, nurses form a half-circle at foot of the bed. Laughing, smiling, talking. "You look so much better than you did in ER!"

Now, three days out from a shower, I surely look homeless. Smile weakly, say whatever pops into my head, "I must have looked pretty bad, if I look better, now." Everyone laughs. They all turn to leave.

Sister and her Friend visit. I can't find my mouth to feed myself. Ventilator gone, but tubes in nose are distracting. Where does the spoon go? Sister feeds me green beans and lasagna. How embarrassing.

Friend asks, "What is that wire for?"

Wire? I reach up, pinch the wire with fingers, and follow it down to body. It disappears under the neck of my hospital gown. "Don't show me!" He turns his head, closes his eyes, puts his hand up, "Stop!" All laugh. Now curious, I look to see. Wire is taped to chest. Something about the heart, no doubt.

Why do the lips hurt to smile? Why does the mouth hurt to chew? Sister passes me a mirror, lets me see bruises on face; cracked, bloody lips; shredded, raw cheeks. What happened? Sister, the only one I can ask, seems clueless like me. She gets scolded for handing me a mirror. Hide the truth from the Mom. Hide her body. Hide her baby. Hide life. Don't let her know.

Have I been in a coma?

No, they say. Fully alert the whole time. Sister says I didn't even sound groggy. Pastor says he visited yesterday, and we laughed so hard it hurt my chest.

Coach says I ask a lot of questions that I don't remember. "Am I pretty? Would you marry me again? Do you love me more than gun magazines?" Over and over, the same questions.

He turns the tables and asks, "Would you marry *me* again?"

Coach says I pause and weigh an answer. Then, "Yes, but I would sure change those wedding vows! I wouldn't give you so many loopholes!"

Three days of my life are lost. I hope I didn't do anything stupid; embarrassing. Can someone fill me in?

But *no-one* wants to talk about Baby Boy. When I ask, eyes lower, faces fall. They turn away and mumble. They don't want to talk. I've never played this game before. Who is on my side? Don't want to make people feel awkward. I'll just wait. Never mind them. I will find out for myself. I will stay with Baby Boy at NICU. Friends have done it. Other people had babies there. The Mom stays till the baby comes home. No problem.

Bring me a pump. Must get my milk supply ready. I will take care of him. It can't be that bad. Coach sends a picture of Baby Boy for me to see. Fully formed, Baby Boy has all his body parts, looks perfectly fine. Some extra tubes and wires, like me, but no missing parts. Coach stays with Baby in NICU. Foggy brain doesn't think to call him or anyone else on the hospital phone. The walls offer no information. No one will talk. Plenty of time here to think troubled thoughts and pray troubled prayers. Must keep thoughts tucked inside. Don't make people uncomfortable.

I ask OB Doctor, "How is Baby doing?"

"It doesn't look good."

Tears fall. Sobs break. Composure leaves. Speechless Doctor puts one hand on my shoulder, leaves. Nurse follows Doctor with teary eyes. No one knows how my heart is ripping. I want to scream! I want my baby! But, like a senseless nightmare, I can't have him! No one will help me! "Oh, God! I want my baby!"

Encounter with God

OB Doctor finally releases me to go. "What happened?" I ask. "No one will tell me."

OB erupts all his pent-up frustrations. He vows to sue Midwives. If he had been in charge, he says, Baby Boy could have been saved, Mom would have been fine.

OB keeps talking, my mind racing. Jolting thoughts never heard before come unprovoked, unrehearsed. *"God. Has. Forsaken. Me. I trusted the Lord. And. He. Failed. Me."*

Holy Spirit steps in with immediate counter-attack from the book of Job, *"Though He slay me, yet will I trust Him"* (Job 13:15, NKJV).

What does that mean? *"Though He slay me..."*

Even if I had died...I could still trust Him? Is this part of a plan? Does this have a purpose? God knew? God allowed? God is still God? He didn't fail me?

OB talking through my thoughts. Very agitated. Lists what *could* have happened: cardiac arrest? lung collapse? renal failure? "We gave twelve units of blood! Six units of plasma! Human beings only hold eight!"

Another jolt. That close to death? Me? And I didn't know it? Don't remember it?

Desperate Trust

Vision comes strong in my mind. Vast expanse of universe... blackness... planets... stars... infinity... knowledge... The Creator of the endless universe notices one small crumb of a person and holds me in his hand. He carries me past the door of death, keeps me alive, has a purpose. Instantly, I comprehend His Holiness and recoil at my unworthiness. I don't deserve His mercy or His love. I am sinful, ashamed. I need forgiveness.

OB declares, "I will talk to District Attorney and see what action I can take."

Now a new emotion: Guilt. My fault. I chose home birth. Baby Boy's blood is on my hands. No escape from gut-wrenching guilt.

OB leaves. Grandparents arrive. I process aloud, bewildered, confused, "I felt fear, but Coach said it would be OK... I thought I did what God wanted me to do..."

Grandparents defend, ready to fight. "OB is not God! He doesn't know! Other home-births were fine!"

I whisper, "If he dies..." No words. Do Not Say the Words. Just point to self.

Grandparents leave; Coach arrives, already briefed on the situation. "It's not your fault. I'll take the blame. You were under authority."

I brush him off. "Let me confess. Listen to all the things I have done wrong. I don't even deserve to live! Forgive me? Pray with me?"

Tormenting guilt and condemnation threaten to drown me, but Coach has something else to say.

I listen as he carefully recites the speech he came to deliver:

"Here's the deal. Doctors have found no brain activity at all in Baby Boy. They say 'cease heroic measures.' Turn the machines off.

You're going to see Baby Boy today. Hold him, rock him, pray for a miracle.

I'm taking the car seat and diapers.

Today.

He will either go home with us... Or go home with Jesus. But remember, we want God's will, no matter what."

God's peace covers me like a blanket. Grace hands me quiet acceptance. Numbness allows me to answer, "Okay." No tears. No hysteria.

My baby will finally be in my arms.

Today.

NICU Experience

ONE HOUR RIDE to NICU hospital. One hour to think. I need to process. Too many questions. Just ride. Wait till you get there. You'll figure it out.

Hospital has a room for us. Families go here to turn off machines. Too many people here, like it's a birthday party or football game. I tell Coach I want to be alone with Baby Boy. Bonding time. Let me hold him, sing to him, take him, and hide from all the faces. Coach arranges my solitary visit to ICU. The crowd waits in the special room.

I scrub up and enter alone; slow, shaky. I find his bed among many. Someone brings me a chair.

He's gone. I can tell. His body is there, with machines humming and hissing. Petroleum jelly covers his closed eyelids. Limp body tells the story. An empty shell. His spirit is gone. "Why didn't they tell me? Why did they pretend he was alive? He's already gone!"

What to think? What to do? Automatically, I bow my head to pray, but I don't know the words. What are the words?

Social worker instantly arrives from nowhere, interrupts my silence, asks endless annoying questions. "They're ready to move Baby Boy to the Room, now." I walk out, numb. No time alone.

Two Doctors sit at a table in the special family room. I sit on the couch. They ask, "Do you have any questions?"

I stare and scream inside, mute. Where do I start? Family all met with Doctors before. They know everything. I know nothing. I feel betrayed. Gullible, second-born me.

I choke out the words, "What happened?"

Their lips move, but I can't hear them. Too far away. Too many people.

"*When* did it happen? Was he born that way?"

They weren't sure when it happened, but yes - born that way. "There was nothing you could have done."

"Are you sure?"

They shake their heads. Nothing.

"*Why* did it happen?"

Another answer I can't hear. Too inhibited to ask for clarity or repetition, I stare, blank. Doctors leave, and I still don't know. "Lord, help me! I have to know if it's my fault!"

Tubes and wires clutch Baby Boy in a corner bed. I walk around, then start to shiver. Teeth start to chatter; I'm suddenly freezing. Nurse insists I lie down with heated blankets on a couch. I don't want this attention. I'm fine, really. But the blankets help. If anyone wants to talk to me, they sit by my couch.

Sister takes a turn by my side. "You know, we are indestructible until our purpose is finished," she says.

I need to hear this. I receive this. Powerful, Peaceful Knowledge. If Baby Boy's purpose is finished, I cannot keep him alive, no matter what I do. If his purpose is *not* finished, no one can end his life, no matter what they try. Sovereign God. Always in control.

Homegoing

NURSE HELPS FAMILY and friends hold Baby Boy. He must stay plugged in at all times. My little flock arrives and gathers around the crib to see. Nurse helps children count tiny toes and fingers. First-born looks under blankets to see what's up. No one tells children the sad news. Happy children believe Baby Boy is coming home with us later today. Cruel game of pretend. Children play with stuffed bears from Nurse. Brain turned off, I don't even think. I assume they know as much as I know. Children hug good-bye to Mom on couch; leave dancing.

I still want to be alone with Baby Boy. Understanding family all leaves to eat. All but one. One busy Aunt doesn't get the hint. Don't hurt her feelings. Give it up.

All return to room, talking, walking, waiting. When will this end? Who will say, *"It's time."* How can anyone say, *"Now."* Who's in charge?

Nurse interrupts my thoughts. "The decision has been made. Somehow, his breathing tube has dislodged on its own. It will just be a matter of time."

Merciful God has settled the questions, made the decisions. Suddenly, machines are off, tubes are out, wires are gone. Now, slowly, softly, make your way to the corner bassinette. Brother hands Baby Boy to Coach. Coach dresses him in "going home" clothes. We sing "Amazing Grace," "How Great Thou Art," "What a Day That Will Be," many more. Between songs, Nurse checks tiny heart. Still beating. Between songs, we hear loud, rasping attempts to breathe. Nurse promises Baby Boy feels no pain. "Oh, God, let him stop. Stop making that horrible sound!"

Finally, tiny body is quiet. Stethoscope is quiet. Nothing to hear. Second nurse comes in to verify. "He's gone. I'm sorry."

Game over. All move toward door. Escape. Get out and shut the door behind you. It's all over. I move slowly. Last one out, I look back at Baby Boy. Motionless form lying on the bed; blanket covering small baby face. Words from God speak to my spirit, allowing me to move. "That's not him. It's an empty shell. You're not leaving him here. He's already in Heaven. Happy."

"… absent from the body … present with the Lord" (2 Cor 5:8).

Funeral

OB SENDS ME to Grandparents' house so Nurse/Grandmother can keep watch. No one sleeps much. 6:00 a.m. – milk lets down. Milk for No Baby. Searing realization hits: Baby Boy is gone. Wails come loud, people come running. Unbearable pain escapes with choking sobs. "How can everyone just go on and forget about him, as if he never existed?!"

Grandmother assures, "No, we won't forget him. Never will the sun set on a day that we haven't thought about him."

Someone has to make funeral arrangements. Not me. Too wobbly, sore and swollen. Coach, Brother, and Uncle take the honors. Three men shop for clothes for Baby Boy to wear to his funeral. They pick a red union suit. Why not.

"What songs will be sung?" They want to know. I remember a Beautiful Song by a Beautiful Lady at a different funeral. But she doesn't know me. Who else could sing it?

"I know her. I'll call her right now," Brother says.

Brother relays, "The Lord had already prepared her heart and asked her to sing it for you. She has heard about Baby Boy. She says yes."

God the Provider. He knows. He sees. He cares. He moves in the hearts of people.

Beautiful Lady sings Beautiful Song. Peaceful. Inspiring. Restful.

Standing in the Presence of the King (Goodman 1990)
    Today I found myself in a most unusual place
    All at once, I was standing face to face
    With someone I knew so well, but I had never seen.
    I was standing in the presence of the King.

    Standing in the presence of the King!
    The world just slips away beneath my feet.
    And mortal man could never write the song that my heart sings
    When I'm standing in the presence of the King.

    Through His gates with thanksgiving,
    Into His courts with praise,
    With a joyful heart, I began to sing.
    For at last, I am standing where he said that I could be.
    I am standing in the presence of the King.

"O Death, where is your sting? O Grave, where is your victory?" (1 Cor 15:55, MKJ)

Dreams

FRIENDS AND RELATIVES all go home. I go home. Grandmother stays on the couch with broken family. Cracked ribs will not allow me to lie down. Must sit up in recliner and stare for six weeks. Breathing hurts. I wade through Psalms on miserable nights. I circle special verses with red pen. All Psalms speak to me. Red circles everywhere.

Dozing in fits and starts, dreams and prayers come alive. I wake up hearing a loud voice, "I want my baby." Was I praying? Wishing? Hoping maybe someone would give him back to me? Quick glance at Grandmother – Is she awake? Does she hear me? Be quiet. He can't come back. That was a stupid thing to say.

Nurse says vivid dreams are common: *Baby Boy is screaming, and I can't find him. Hurry and hunt! He needs me! I see his leg sticking out from under a pile of blankets! I throw blankets in every direction. Keep throwing, there's more! Unending pile of blankets! I can't reach him! He's crying!*

I wake up exhausted, overwhelmed, grieving deeper. There are no blankets. There is no baby.

Mind processes at night. *I hear Baby Boy crying. Someone is running away with him, stealing him! Run hard after them, keep screaming, "Stop!" They might hear. I might catch them!* But I never do.

Dreams evolve. *Now I'm holding Baby Boy tight, running. Some unseen foe is after us. We must hide in caves. They will try to take Baby Boy.*

Tormenting dreams never end. Nurse says some mothers need medication to sleep. The mother/child bond is fierce, unbreakable.

I see a scripture: "But Jesus said, 'Let the little children come to me and do not try to stop them'" (Mt 19:14 NET). I am hanging onto Baby Boy in my heart and forbidding him to go to Jesus. I must release him in my spirit. Let him go. Place him, once more, on a deeper level, in loving arms of the Perfect Father who will take perfect care. When I let him go, crazy dreams stop.

"Children are an inheritance from the Lord" (Ps 127:3, GW). If He gave me Baby Boy in the first place, I can hand him back, for safe-keeping.

Guilt

CAUSE AND EFFECT parenting. That's my lifestyle. Wrong behavior brings consequences.

"You cut your foot because you went barefoot when I told you to wear shoes."

"The window is broken because you threw the ball in the house."

"You're in trouble because you disobeyed."

Bad begets bad. So...why did Baby Boy die? Did I do something wrong? Go back through pregnancy; look for failure. *Aha*! Bad attitude the week before birth! That's it! No, that can't be it. *Think, think*! What could it be? Cry out to God driving down the road, "What did I do wrong?!"

Helpful Nurse keeps calling every week and checking. She asks, "Do you feel guilty when your other children fall and get hurt, have accidents?"

"Yes, I do! If I had been watching more closely, it wouldn't have happened!"

False guilt. False responsibility. Nurse says, "Call it an accident. An unfortunate accident." Accidents have no one to blame.

Jack Hayford's book, *I'll Hold You in Heaven*, (1990, p. 89), says guilt is Satan's way of clawing at the wounds of grief. Sister agrees, "If guilt is true, confess it. If guilt is false, reject it."

I tell God everything: "I feel guilty for...*this*, and *this*, and *this*. If any of it contributed to Baby Boy's death, then I deserve to die."

But Jesus already died for me in my place! He took the punishment for all my faults, real or imaginary. Thank God all mistakes were paid for on the cross. Someone died. So I can go on living.

"There is therefore now no condemnation for those who are in Christ Jesus" (Rom 8:1).

Questions

FRIEND COUNSELS, "ASK *God* why He let it happen, instead of asking yourself."

Do we get to question God? Is that right or wrong?

Friend says, "We need to think His thoughts. We have to ask Him for a reason to rejoice so we can 'give thanks in everything' (1 Thes 5:18), and 'rejoice in the Lord always' (Phil 4:4). Don't demand an explanation; just ask for His point of view."

Cautiously, expectantly, I pray, "God, why did you allow this to happen?"

Next day, walking through the house, I catch a phrase from a radio preacher: "What does God do with sacrifices?"

Preacher answers himself, "He burns them."

Flashback ... four years ago: Special prayer. Special sacrifice. Offer my body to God to use as He pleases. Complete surrender. What will He do? I assume He'll use my body for mass reproduction - maybe thirteen kids? Doesn't look like it, now. He plans something I couldn't know, wouldn't guess. He takes my body to the grave and back to show His power. He burns it.

God burns sacrifices to purify them and bring to nothing that which we claim as ours. He burns sacrifices to show His acceptance of them. God accepts my offering and uses it in a way He designs. And He gets the glory.

I learn things from the fire. No need to fear death. I'm indestructible until my purpose is finished. Lazarus can't be threatened with death. He laughs at death.

I learn about people who were brought to prayer for me. To their knees. To their faces. To the throne. When people pray, they draw closer to God. Some take off work. Some turn to God. Some turn from lukewarm to dedicated. People, who barely know me, hear in passing. Crying out to God for me. Revival. Not in churches, but in gas stations, living rooms, closets. For many years, I yearn to be used by God, but how can He use me if I never go to a far-off jungle to preach? All I have to offer Him is a life already His: my "reasonable service" (Rom 12:1b). He takes a scrawny housewife and brings results that I cannot orchestrate.

I may never see how the fire "works together for good" (Rom 8:28), but I have to trust God to make it happen. "Blessed are those who do not see, and yet believe" (Jn 20:29, paraphrased).

Decisions

SIX WEEK CHECK-UP proves to be everything I dread. Nurse hands a little paper gown to me, and I get dizzy, lean against the wall for support. Exposure is not my forte, no matter how many eyes have already seen.

OB Doctor says, "I've decided not to sue midwives."

Relief loosens tense muscles, somewhat.

However," OB continues, "Don't go around telling folks that homebirths are OK, because they are not. But, don't feel guilty! You didn't know any better and had no money; you did the best you could."

He doesn't know we have college degrees and insurance. One more thing to forgive.

"Now," OB declares, "We need to tie your tubes. You have five children. That should be enough."

Tie your tubes?? So crass - like I'm a dog.

Do his words change my convictions? Mental review: God opens and closes the womb. God has all power and all wisdom. Dare I declare, "I don't trust you anymore, God. You don't know what you're doing. I'll handle this reproduction thing from now on, thanks."

Unanticipated boldness speaks to OB, "We gave our family size to God. We let Him decide. My vision has always been a large family, and my heart is still there."

OB hears me. "So the spirit is willing, but the flesh is weak?" (Mt 26:41).

How did he know that verse? I agree and assure OB I'm not going to make any big decisions at this point.

OB sighs, shakes his head, "I don't understand that kind of faith."

I don't understand it, either. Don't have to. Just take each day as it comes. Trust God to allow only those things into my life that will be for my good and His glory.

Faith may wobble. Trust may shake. But God remains faithful (2 Tim 2:13, HCSB). He is Who He is.

Heart Pain

If I could have another baby, it will surely heal the pain. But Coach says wait two years. OB says never. For now, I will hold other people's babies. Every baby I see. That will help. Wrong! One baby, belonging to another mother, does nothing. No salve. No enjoyment. No connection.

If my other children, ones that I birthed, don't take away the pain, how could another child, even another from my own body? If the joy of sunshine, flowers, and cool breezes do not take the pain, how can the joy of another baby erase the pain of a loss?

There's no way to end this pain without Baby Boy in my arms! I believe this lie. No hope of healing in this life. Hopeless depression creeps in. Huge, dull grey depression looms large. Baby Boy won't come back.

I cry when I'm alone. How long? Six months? The sadness won't leave. Coach nudges, "Have you thanked God for what happened? Not thank God that it could have been worse, but thank God for exactly what happened, in exactly the way it happened?"

I know the Bible says, "In everything give thanks" (1 Thes 5:18). But it feels wrong. Thank God for Baby Boy's death? I don't want to. I refuse to.

Lie says, "Stay sad if you care about Baby Boy. You can't be happy if you really love him. You shouldn't."

What does God say? "Weeping may endure for a night, but Joy comes in the morning" (Ps 30:5b NKJV).

Try it. Try to obey the Word. List "benefits" of the whole crazy ordeal. Think hard. Pray. Eight benefits emerge on notebook paper. List of benefits forces my focus to shift. I thank God that He is here. He knows how it hurts.

In prayer, I climb up on His lap and pour my broken heart out to Him. Let Him wrap me in the folds of His robe, hide me under His wings (Ps 17:8, NASB), hold me till the pain is gone - till He makes it all better, like a perfect Father would do for the wounds of life. Give God the pain and the sadness, and let Him carry it for me. Let Him kiss my tears away. Grey cloud begins to lift.

Acceptance. IT IS. Forever woven into the fabric of my life. Memories leave a lasting imprint, but Jesus carries the pain (Is 53:4).

Comfort

THOUGHTS SLIDE TOO easily into despair. Make another list. This time, list comforting thoughts. Thoughts that will crowd out the sadness of my empty arms.

1. Baby Boy is where I want all my children to eventually be - Heaven. Baby Boy just arrives first.
2. He is safe. No chance to live a life of rebellion.
3. He is perfectly cared for. Getting plenty of milk, sleep, stimulation. Never sick with colic.
4. He will never be yelled at or beat up by bullies. Never made fun of or teased. Never be confused about the prejudices or wickedness of men.
5. The first face he saw was the face of Jesus. Breathtaking! Beautiful!
6. Precious in the sight of the Lord is the death of His saints (Ps 116:15).
7. We will *all* have to die, someday. He couldn't live forever.
8. I will see him in Heaven and get to hold him for as long as I want. We will pick up where life was interrupted.

Whenever my heart begins to ache, I grab my comfort list and read it. The heart drifts Heavenward. Peace settles in.

"He gives us comfort in all our troubles. Then we can comfort other people who have the same troubles" (2 Cor 1:4, NLT).

Another Baby?

COACH CALLS A Time-Out, stalling. "Let your body heal," he says. "Wait two years."

Wait? How do we do that? Self-control and deference, I naively believe. I investigate Natural Family Planning. This is fascinating stuff! I've never tried all these charts! Never knew these signs of fertility! Four-tenths of a Fahrenheit degree indicates ovulation. My life dangles on four-tenths of a degree. I must read the thermometer very carefully, chart very carefully. Now, sleep with one eye open.

"It's not your day, Coach! Look at the chart! Read the chart!"

Very tense two years. I fear for my very life. Nerves are shot. Do I even want to risk another pregnancy, anyway?

I know! I'll adopt! I Begin to fantasize about finding a baby on my doorstep.

"Now, Lord, let's talk about this. You know that the only reason I want more children is to teach them about you and train them in the ways of God," I make my petition.

Instantly, a picture flashes into my mind – A confused little eight-year-old girl with no home. I know her.

"What about this one?" the Lord is asking, waiting for a response from me.

"That's not what I meant, Lord (years later, I will *really* regret this.)."

Picture disappears. Who am I kidding? I want a baby for *myself*; to cuddle, to nurse, to adore, and to adore *me*. It's all about *me*. Stop faking noble motives! Don't even think about adoption again. It would be for the wrong reasons.

Two years almost over, and Coach comes home from work sick. Every day. Boss says he can't come back to work without a doctor's note. Doctor sends Coach to the hospital – Diabetes. Coach slogs home after three days with insulin shots morning and evening. For the rest of his life. Recovers slowly, painfully. Neuropathy in legs; everything hurts. Socks hurt. Air hurts. Don't even touch him.

Standing beside very sick Coach, I chirp, "It's been two years!"

Coach eye-rolls, "You have got to be kidding."

Adverse effects of diabetes prevent conception. Throw charts away; no need. Is God protecting me? Can He be trusted? He proves again He is wise enough to make these decisions. He is all-knowing.

"O Lord, you examine me and know me. You know when I sit down and when I get up; even from far away you understand my motives. You carefully observe me when I travel or when I lie down to rest; you are aware of everything I do" (Ps 139: 1-3, NET).

Searching

ELIZABETH GEORGE, IN *Loving God with All Your Mind* (1994), says Old World Painters paint the canvas black before beginning a masterpiece. It gives depth to the colors and beauty to the painting.

I see it. God has painted my world black. There's sadness, fear, marriage strain, stress. Maybe God has a masterpiece in mind. Could there be something beautiful to look forward to?

Sunday School flashback: When Shadrach, Meshach, and Abednego are thrown into the fiery furnace, they come out none the worse, even a little better. The only things that burn are the ropes that bind their hands and feet. The fire loosens them from whatever hinders them before. And they don't even smell like smoke.

God, shield me from the smoke of bitterness and despair.

Keep searching. For peace, help, sanity. Books, Bibles, biographies - some help more than others. Never stop searching.

I study Fanny Crosby: Christian songwriter *extraordinaire* from the 1800's, a physician's error leaves Baby Fanny blind. She discovers later the guilt and regret the mistaken doctor carries. Fanny expresses, "If I could talk to him now, I would tell him, 'Thank you, thank you, thank you for making me blind!'"

Her handicap renders her completely free of distractions, free of the world's siren song. Blindness makes her devoted to and dependent upon the unseen.

I need to go one step further with my forgiveness. Errors happen, but God is bigger. He allows them for a reason. I need to forgive, but not just forgive. I must be able to say in my heart to everyone involved, "Thank you, thank you, thank you for your part in this tragedy!" Oh, how hard! The words come out in gulps and sobs, but I do it by faith. Anger falls off. Gone.

When everything is shaken that can be shaken, nothing is left but the Rock.

Scripture speaks to me, "That I may know Him, and the power of His resurrection, and the fellowship of His sufferings…" (Phil 3:10). Two ways to know the Lord: victorious mountaintop power, and heart-wrenching suffering. Through intense anguish, I now identify with His suffering. My suffering is small compared to His, but I know Him in a new way. Deeper.

This "fellowship of suffering" draws me to other mothers who ache over babies gone. We cry together. Strangers become friends through sharing grief: in grocery stores, restaurants, campgrounds; holy places, all. But with believers, we share more. We know resurrection is coming. This pain will give way to unspeakable Joy. These ashes will be traded for breath-taking Beauty. This heaviness will be lifted with a shout of praise (Is 61:3)! For believers, the best is yet to come!

Hidden Pain

MIDDLE BROTHERS, ALWAYS together. Laughing, running, happy cohorts in crime. Lanky One reads directions. Stocky One slams a hammer. Lanky One instructs, hand to shoulder; Stocky One nods his head. Twins not in age, but in heart, dressed alike.

But six weeks after Baby Boy passes, when I'm back in my bed at night, no more recliner, Happy Middle Brothers come crying together to my room at 2:30 a.m. LOUD.

"What's wrong?"

"We don't know!"

Do they have the same bad dream at the same bad time? I make them a pallet by my bed. Rule book says don't ever let children sleep with you. Ever. You'll ruin them. You'll never get them out of your bed. Never. I follow the rules and make pallets for sobbing middle brothers. Night after night for a week, maybe two. Coach says, "I'll make the pallets before we go to bed. Then we're ready for them at 2:30." Great idea.

Then they stop coming.

Years later, with the condemnation of hindsight, I moan. "Boys, I'm so sorry I didn't take you in my arms and hold you close to snuggle in my bed and kiss away the hurt. Should have followed my heart instead of the rule book. " I should have, at the very least, prayed with them. But at 2:30 a.m., I only think of myself. I focus inward. I'm tired.

They don't remember their 2:30 tears, but I do.

Were there any rule books on "How to Help Brothers Deal with Death"? Would I have read them? I find out too late: death in the family makes children fear. "Whatever happened to Baby Brother could happen to me. Will I be next? Am I safe? Is anyone safe?"

Another child endures terrifying nightmares. Everyone is dying in his dreams. He tells no one. He doesn't want to add to Little Mama's pain. Looking on, no one knew his secret agony, his dread of sleep. Extreme pain calls for extreme measures. Self-preservation causes him to shut down all feelings of love for siblings. If he doesn't love them, it won't hurt so much when they die. Replace fear with hate. Hate everyone.

Most of the children believe for many years their parents *choose* to leave Baby Boy at the hospital. Parents don't want him for some reason? Won't try to save him. Abandon him. They believe this because no one talks about it. How tragic. I just assume they understand. Of course, they don't understand. No one understands.

If I could go back, make it right, what would I do?

One-on-one listening. Plan a whole day with each child individually. Ask questions. Pray. Comfort. Love. "Weep with those who weep" (Rom 12:15, HCSB).

Get a third party who isn't emotionally involved. Someone with discernment to help expose the lies and discover the truth (See Reference page). Truth brings freedom (Jn 8:32).

Desperate Trust

So sorry, sweet children. So many mistakes. So tangled up in my own grief, I couldn't see your silent suffering. Forgive me?

Lord, show them my heart, my imperfect love. I can't go back, but You can. You span time. You *Are*. Show them You are still there, and You care. Hold them for me. Heal their pain.

How Big is God?

ANALYTICAL PEOPLE NEED to put things in boxes and label the boxes. I try hard to answer all the questions and close the box of "Baby Boy" so I can go on. Give the box a label and put it on a shelf. Done.

But this box won't close. Too many "Whys" and "Wherefores". Like a jigsaw puzzle with pieces missing. *Someone*, please tell me everything I said and everything that happened! It drives me crazy! But no one wants me to ask. They go on with their quiet life, but I still need to process. It would make them uncomfortable for me to ask. Especially now. It has been so long. But I can't close the box with empty spaces left!

And something else I can't understand. GOD. I want to bring Him down to my level, so He can explain this whole aching event to me. But I must bow to the fact that I can't understand Him. His wisdom is far past my ability to comprehend (Rom 11:33). Even if He explains it to me. Like a third grader in a Nuclear Physics class. "As the heavens are higher than the earth, so are my ways higher than your ways and my thoughts than your thoughts" (Is 55:9). I give.

When I demand to understand, I put my intellect on the throne of my life. "If I can understand it, I will accept it."

God says, "Accept it with your spirit, whether or not you understand it. Walk by faith, not by sight" (2 Cor 5:7). God alone is sovereign, and His will governs all.

Homeschool flashback: just prior to Baby Boy accident, we study Humility: God is so big; we are so small, like breadcrumbs. We all pray, "God, show us how big you are. Amen."

How Big? Bringing the dead back to life is Really Big. If a body doesn't breathe or have a pulse for forty-five minutes, it is clinically dead (that would be me). How much bigger can God get?

Thank you, God, for being so big that nothing is impossible for you, even though that makes you too big to put in a box.

Reginald Heber writes "Holy, Holy, Holy" in 1861. Many years later, it teaches, encourages, comforts.

> Holy, holy, holy! Though the darkness hide Thee.
> Though the eyes of sinful man Thy glory may not see.
> Only Thou art holy; there is none beside Thee.
> Perfect in power, in love, and purity.

Ministry

CHRISTMAS CANDLE-LIGHTING SERVICE at the hospital, and the whole family is invited. The whole family does not want to go. Too much. Too soon. Grandmother goes with me.

Unfamiliar with this type of service, we go anyway, hoping to find a balm for the gaping wounds of grief. We watch and listen as names of babies are read from a list, and a candle is lit for each baby who died here, in this hospital. Five years' worth of names. A prayer is recited for each one. Some songs are sung.

We see a huge Christmas tree bedecked with fabric angels, each bearing the name of a departed baby. We get to take our fabric angel home. It doesn't heal, but it is something to hold.

I look out over a sea of people representing a club I do not want to join. They are the Grieving Parents. Before the Accident, I would not have talked to them. Would not have known what to say. Now I know. Don't say anything. Just listen. Let them do all the talking.

Sympathetic keynote speaker comments, "I would love to be able to hear all of your stories."

Me! I want to tell my story! To anyone who will listen. Every time I tell it, the telling gets a little easier. Even if I cry, a measure of healing is in the telling. Sharing Baby Boy's story is sharing his life, his memory. They will remember him, too. I need to tell, and when they listen, it brings comfort.

Is this a calling? A mission field? A ministry I would never choose for myself – but doesn't God use our weaknesses for His glory?

"Would you write a note to a co-worker who recently lost a baby?" Pops wants to know. Yes, I will.

"Will you talk to my cousin who just lost a baby?" Lady at church wants to know. Sure, I will.

I pass along the comfort of God to other hurting people. We make it through by God's grace, reflecting the glory of God into the darkness of grief, lighting a path for others to follow.

"Blessed be …the God of all comfort, who comforts us in all our tribulation, that we may be able to comfort them which are in any trouble, by the comfort wherewith we ourselves are comforted of God" (2 Cor 1:3-4).

Anniversary

I DRAG THE entire family, flowers in hand, to the cemetery on the first anniversary of Baby Boy's death. What will we do there? Who knows? I brought my Bible, just in case.

Van conversation with little Pinky Dinky goes like this:

"Are we taking these flowers to Baby Boy?"

"Not exactly. We're taking them to the cemetery."

"Does he live at the cemetery?"

"No, he lives in Heaven."

"Are we going to Heaven to give them to Baby Boy?"

"No, we're going to the cemetery."

"When will we get to Baby Boy's house?"

Remind me again why we are going to the cemetery. It seems silly, now. Kids, off leash, run willy-nilly picking up stray flowers, making dirty, faded bouquets.

Coach doesn't want to be here. He snorts, "Put the flowers back! Stop running!"

Pinky Dinky wanders aimlessly among the markers, swinging flowers at her side, mumbling, "Where is Baby Boy?"

I watch. Silent. The Holy Spirit nudges, "Why seek ye the living among the dead? He is not here for He is risen" (Mt 28:6). The same words the angel speaks to the women at Jesus' empty tomb. The same power that raises Jesus from the dead raises Baby Boy to live with Him. No need to visit him at the cemetery. No one here.

"Let's load up, kids. We'll see him in Heaven." I smile; I picture myself holding, rocking, loving Baby Boy. Not today. Not here. But soon enough.

Monument

COACH SAYS GRAVE marker will cost five hundred dollars. Five hundred squeaky dollars later, the overworked dishwasher needs replaced. Goodbye, dollars. We pinch together five hundred more bucks, and the exhausted washing machine gives up the ghost. On and on. Eighteen months roll by. Every attempt to save money gets eaten up by life, and no monument for Baby Boy's grave.

Busy life with five little people. Pinky Dinky has eczema and allergies and cries all the time. I make plans to pray all night, face to the floor, for Pinky Dinky's healing. Jesus prayed all night. So can I.

Lights go out, children asleep, sick Coach sleeping in recliner tonight, I hit the bedroom floor. I pray, "Lord, I would take her eczema for her!"

He says, "I already took it – on the cross."

Silence. What is He saying? What does that mean?

Scriptures float through my mind, unbidden. Slowly, one verse at a time, hidden in the heart long ago.

"Ask and it shall be given you, seek and ye shall find, knock and it shall be opened unto you" (Mt 7:7).

> *"Whatsoever you shall ask the Father in my name, He will give it you"* (Jn 16:23).
> *"If you abide in me and my words abide in you, you shall ask what you will and it will be done for you"* (Jn 15:7).

Wait a minute. These aren't my thoughts. Not me straining my brain to dig up prayer promises. "Lord, are you trying to tell me something? Are you telling me she is healed? All I have to do is ask?"

Silence. How will I know? Healings sometimes come gradually - might not see it right away. Don't lose faith if God is doing something. I need a sign. Hezekiah asks for a sign of his healing, and God gives it (2 Kings 20:8).

"Father, if you are saying 'yes,' please verify it with a monument for Baby Boy. That will be my sign."

Peace. Joyful, expectant hope in my heart, I climb into bed with a smile – no need to stay up all night and pray. I already have my answer. Just wait. Watch.

Up before dawn, unaware of my evening prayer vigil, Coach announces, "I sold that old, broken car for five hundred dollars. You can use the money for Baby Boy's grave marker."

I laugh and leap. Coach thinks I'm crazy.

Monument Company sends a mock-up and estimate for what I want. Total comes to... $499.75. God not only supplies, He supplies just enough.

Monument ready in a few weeks. They call and say, "Meet us at the cemetery today."

I groan. This is the day Sister comes home from the hospital with her new baby girl. I want to meet New Baby at her home, not the monument at the cemetery. I have plans for New Baby to be my "lovie." But duty rules and cemetery wins. New Baby will have to wait.

Headstone in place, I drive away from the cemetery, thoughtful, slow. The Holy Spirit teaches, "Sister has *her* baby. You have *yours*. Your baby is in a different place, but fully alive. This is *your* life. This is *your* ministry. This cemetery is part of My plan for you."

God is not fair. God chooses a different path for Sister and me. And everyone else. Fairness gives everyone the same thing, whether or not they need it or deserve it. Justice gives everyone what they need or deserve, even if they don't want it. Can't appreciate it at the time. God gives both Sister and me what we need to fulfill our purposes on earth. And He never makes mistakes.

The Test

THREE YEARS OUT from the *Accident*, and I'm sure I'm pregnant. I have all the symptoms: late, queasy, tired.

Now what?

Panic! Mind screaming, "OhGodohGodohGod! Notagain! Notagain!" It's not my own death that I fear – I have already faced that. But what if another baby dies? Too much for the brain to hold. I can't think. Can't pray.

No sleep for days. What happened to faith? Do I trust Him or not? Possibility of pregnancy reveals very tiny faith, indeed. Fear threatens to suffocate me.

Night number three of staring into darkness repeating, "OhGodohGod," the still small voice of my Lord interrupts me.

"Didn't I carry you?"

"Yes, Lord."

"Didn't I do what was best?"

Slight hesitation. "Yes, Lord, you always do what is best, even if I don't like it or understand it."

"Can you trust me to do what is best, again?"

Long hesitation. What is He asking me? Go through the fire again? I mentally survey all the events of Baby Boy's birth, delivery, death, public scrutiny, humiliation, misunderstandings. I emotionally relive the whole thing. Ambulances, blood. All bad. All to be avoided…

God is waiting for an answer.

…On the other hand, I *do* want to be used by God. What else does life offer? Coast into eternity slowly, safely, quietly; the world unaffected by my life? Unaware that I was even here?

I wrestle with the question and the answer. Much thinking later, I envision a lamb following its shepherd. No hesitations, it knows that in the shepherd's presence, there is no real danger. Complete trust. Just follow.

Surrender. Let go. Of everything. Let go of pride, control, dignity, reputation, safety, comfort, life. Release.

I answer in the darkness, "Alright, Lord. If it is your perfect plan… and if it will benefit your Kingdom to take me through that again… every painful detail… I'll do it for you. You love me. You see the end from the beginning (Is 46:10). You know what is best for me. I will follow you like a lamb follows the Shepherd (Ps 23)."

The peace of God that passes all understanding (Phil 4:7) comes over me, and I sleep like a baby. No worries.

New morning. Not pregnant after all. Was it just a test? Midnight encounter with God dispels all fear. Like a sheep, I'll go with Him all the way.

Mysteries

FIVE YEARS COME and go since Baby Boy leaves. Five children growing up. Busy days. Busy lives. Give away baby clothes and maternity clothes. "Look at the bright side," I tell myself, "It won't be long till I can give away giant piles of toys! Clean house! More room!"

I meet a lady at a conference who is grieving the loss of a baby. Her aching heart and empty arms will never hold another newborn, the doctor says. I share my story with her, telling her JOY can come, even *without* another baby. I share how God replaces the yearning to have more children with a restful peace. "Just keep trusting and giving everything in your heart to God," I say.

I don't realize at that moment a tiny speck of a baby is listening from the inside.

Weeks later, I notice the calendar. "I'm late!" I report to Coach, wide eyed.

"You're just getting old. Those things happen to women your age."

Forty is old? But one week later, I try a home pregnancy test, my first ever. Heart skips a beat – it's positive!

"That's impossible!" Coach doesn't believe the test. He believes his diabetes permanently ends any ability to father more children. Many theories are being disproven here. Let's keep it quiet for a while.

Maybe we're dreaming. What if we aren't? What will the relatives say? They all think we "did something about it" years ago. Everyone will think we are crazy. Truth be told, they probably already think that. They'll think we're completely *stupid*. They'll think...

"Coach, what will people think?!" I keep asking. Pride overshadows any medical concerns.

"Let them think what they want to think! I'm excited! This is a miracle!"

I don't dampen his enthusiasm. Alone, I ask my Lord how to view this news. "Should I approach it with grave concern and somber face, like a cancer diagnosis? Or be excited, like a regular pregnancy, where nothing goes wrong?"

The Holy Spirit answers, "Rejoice in the Lord always, and again I say rejoice" (Phil 4:7).

Of course! I should rejoice no matter what the outcome will be! Break out the dancing shoes! A baby is on the way!

The Announcement

Now, how exactly do we tell the relatives? Put it off as long as possible. They don't know about my midnight encounter with the voice of God years before. They only know fear. They don't have the grace of God on every step of this secret pregnancy. They remember the shadow of death.

Coach doesn't agree with hiding the news. He thinks all will share his excitement. He believes Baby is a special blessing from God to heal the pain from our loss. Coach is eager to be called "Abraham," but finally agrees to keep my secret till the belly shouts, "Pregnant!"

But Coach can't wait to spill the beans. He tells kids the big news, "So they can start praying about it."

All are excited but one. First-born is very apprehensive about another pregnancy. He remembers more than the others. But keeping a secret makes it fun, so all agree to wait till Family Picnic on the 4th of July. We'll call it the "Big Bang!"

We chicken out on 4th of July. So, the next day, we let the kids make phone calls. Speaker phone betrays hesitant answers, incredulous answers, silent answers. We hang up and laugh. The cat is out of the bag!

Now, to find a doctor. Midwife won't touch me with a ten-foot pole. Coach says doctor and hospital must be close to home – no long drives this time. I find no local female doctors, no blind male ones, either. Prayerfully pick a clinic.

All tests are good – the perfect patient. I exercise, drink carrot juice, take naps. Ultrasound declares, "It's a boy!" Pinky Dinky cries for days. She wants a sister.

Coach crows, "This baby will have a special purpose! He will be the next George Washington!"

Another day, "He will be the next Abraham Lincoln!"

Then, "The next Billy Graham! The next Einstein!" Whatever Baby becomes, it will be BIG, according to Coach.

Isaac should be his name. It means "laughter." Every time I share the news, we all laugh. Perfect name. But every family member has more suggestions. They fire names at me all day. "Reuben! Christopher! Samuel! Jonathan! Jacob!" They address my belly by their name of choice, then hug and caress the belly to make the name stick. We make a list, and I promise to consider every name. But *Isaac* is perfect.

Siblings-to-be pile toys in a corner of my room. Where will we put this baby? "If there is room in the heart, there is room in the home," the old saying goes. Friends are planning a shower, and then, *really*, where will we put it?

Next, maternity clothes. For a forty-year-old? No way! Shop resale for yesteryear's maternity clothes – when women hid belly buttons under tent-like dresses. My style.

Prayers

SEVEN YEAR-OLD PINKY-DINKY says, "When the baby comes, I will hold him like this…I will burp him like this…I will snuggle him like this…."

Eleven year-old Lanky One excitedly shares, "Every now and then I think I dreamed that we were going to have a baby; then, I realize: it's real! We really *are* going to have a baby!"

I sit down with God one day for a heart to heart talk. "I know You've got this," I say. "I know whatever happens, it will be for the best, but if I just knew what lay ahead, good or bad, I could prepare myself."

Holy Spirit speaks, "I will never leave you, nor forsake you" (Heb 13:5).

That's all I need to know. If He goes with me, I can go through anything.

Tests show high thyroid numbers. Doctor says we need another test, then take medication if it is still high. I don't like medication. It's not natural. Especially while pregnant. I look in nursing handbook and find thyroid meds during pregnancy mean no breastfeeding. Horrors! Babies without breastfeeding? Unthinkable! Let's pray!

I call a prayer warrior with a healing ministry. He says fear might play a part here. Fear is not of God. He shares a list of scriptures about fear and suggests I read them aloud whenever I feel worried, nervous, or fearful. "Eventually, you will believe what you are reading, and it will change you."

I take the list of verses to bed at night with a flashlight. Nighttime, when sleep plays hard-to-get, when fears and worries grow large, I read verses aloud. I memorize them after a time and no longer need the flashlight. Coach tells me, "You talk in your sleep."

I laugh. "I'm awake – just quoting scripture in the dark!"

A book says, "To get rid of disease, get rid of bitterness" (Mk 11:24-26).

"Lord, am I bitter toward anyone?"

Flashback of a time when someone did me wrong. How petty! But I realize I am still miffed about that. I admit bitterness to God, ask Him to forgive me, and reclaim the ground given to the enemy. I go further and ask God to bless the offender. I would rather be healed than carry a grudge.

Second thyroid test is normal! I smile and heave a big sigh of relief. I make plans to call all prayer partners and share the good news; but something interrupts the good news plans.

The Crash

BABY ISN'T MOVING. All day. Sometimes that happens. He'll move when I lie down tonight. But all is still. All night. When Coach wakes up, I ask him to talk to Baby – tell him to move. Coach talks to all our unborn babies, and they listen to his voice. But this time, nothing happens.

I call Doctor, choke on the words to receptionist: Baby hasn't moved for twenty-four hours. She says drink a whole quart of ice-water while lying very still. That should wake him up. But it doesn't.

Drive to Doctor's office. Sit in parking lot. Pray.

"Okay, God, this is serious. If you let this baby live, I'll… I'll… I'll what? (If there is ever a good time to start bargaining with God, this is it.)

I'll…give my body to you? (No, I've already done that.)

I'll…quit my job? (Done that, too.)

I'll…homeschool my children? (Done.)

I'll…go anywhere you want – Africa? China? (He already knows I'm willing and even anxious to go.)

Think! Think! What can I offer?!

I have no bargaining chips. There is nothing left to offer God except Baby himself. I'm simply at the mercy of God. Surrender, again. "God, my body, my baby, my life, and my dreams are yours. It's up to you."

In the office, familiar nurse smiles, "Let me get a heart tone so you can stop worrying."

Exam room is silent. Hold my breath while she places Doppler here, there, here again. She is determined to find it. Finally, she admits, "I don't know." Sobs break. Hope crashes. Nurse prays aloud while I hide my face under my shirt.

Another nurse tries without success. "But don't worry, yet. Let's get an ultrasound. Sometimes, *blah, blah, blah.*"

Coach meets me at the imaging center. Another silent exam room. Technician takes dozens of pictures of very still Baby. She has one answer to all of our questions: "I cannot diagnose."

We have to return to Doctor's office for the official announcement. "Baby is gone."

Doctor says it's too risky to wait for labor to start naturally. Check into hospital in the morning to be induced.

I must go home first to tell the children. How do we explain something we don't understand?

They know something is wrong. Word has spread. Preacher is here. Relatives are coming.

"Baby is gone."

Pinky Dinky is most vocal. "Why, mama?"

"We don't know, honey."

"But, why, mama?" Her troubled face intently searches my eyes for a clue. There *has* to be a reason!

"We don't know."

"But, *why*?" She begs to understand.

No answers.

Delivery

GATHER THINGS FOR the hospital, like packing to go to prison camp. I don't want to go, but I have no choice. My mind goes into auto-pilot. Don't think.

I force my feet to walk across the hospital parking lot, zombie-fashion. Repeat with every step, "I will never leave you nor forsake you" (Heb 13:5). "Lo, I am with you always, even till the end of the world" (Mat 28:20).

Labor is a nightmare, baby or no baby. Induction is wicked - contractions off the chart; worst ever. Keep giving more pain meds till fitful sleep takes over. Blood pressure drops to 50/30. Breathing stops several times. Monitor beeps. Someone shakes me and says, "Breathe!"

I insist, "I *am* breathing!"

Pain and drugs are fighting for control. Pain is winning. Desperation cries out, "God, help me!" Over and over. Nurse asks Coach to move from my side to corner of the room. He's not on home turf. Not in the game. Not ready. No one is ready. It's too soon. Pain intensifies. Out of control. Game starts without us. Nurses stand like wooden soldiers at either side of the foot of the bed. They don't move; don't speak; just stare. Torture scene from a horror movie? What is happening?

New thought: If Coach were here, in my face, what would he say? I see him in my mind, eyes wide, white showing all around the brown, coaching, "Blow! Blow!"

I frantically obey mental image. Start blowing. This distracts me from screaming, but pain escalates.

If Trusty were here, what would she say? I hear her voice saying, "Let's check your dilation. It might be time to push."

I scream at Nurse, "Please check dilation! When can I push?"

Nurse says, "I'll check, but I can't tell you any numbers."

What? Is my dilation a secret? How will I know when to push? Why can't she tell me? Is this how they do things in hospitals?

Nurse leans down, quietly directs, "You can bear down if you want and miscarry right here on the bed." She pats the bed for emphasis.

Sounds like *"Push"* to me! And I am on my own. I may as well deliver on the sidewalk outside, for all the help I receive here. I feel for Baby myself, while nurses stare. "Baby is coming!" If I shout loud enough, she will do something, surely. Finally getting into the action, Nurse wrangles me onto my back (where I don't want to be) and delivers tiny breech Baby. She saves placenta for Doctor.

Later, Doctor and nurse have subdued exchange:

"How did it go?"

"It was easy."

Easy for whom?! So glad it's over, I say nothing.

Retrospection tells me Nurse *wants* to deliver by herself, to add a notch to her belt. She never intends to call Doctor until after the birth. But it has to look like an accident, with no knowledge of dilation, no coaching, no direction to push. Just, "Oops! Here's a baby!"

This plan is so offensive to me, as if my baby and my situation do not warrant a doctor's attention.

(When I phone Nurse, days later, I ask if she had been aware of my history. She says if there had been a problem, she would have grabbed a doctor off the floor. But I don't want a doctor off the floor! I choose my doctor on purpose, after much prayer. Shouldn't she ask if I have a preference? Nurse defends, "I've delivered many fetal demise." No doubt. Always more to forgive. Always.)

Doctor checks placenta; I hold Tiny Baby; Coach cries quiet tears at my side. CD, softly playing scriptures throughout the birth, is finally audible. We hear, "…and God shall wipe away all tears from their eyes, and there shall be no more death, neither sorrow, nor crying, neither shall there be any more pain, for the former things are passed away" (Mt 28:20).

Thank you, God, for directing our thoughts upward. A better world is coming. Babies will reunite with families. We will praise God together at the throne.

Mopping Up

GOWN, BEDDING, PILLOW: all soaked. Disregard it. Nurse throws sheet over all. Folks want to come in. Roomful of relatives who don't know what to say. "How much does he weigh?" They offer sympathies and leave one by one.

Pinky Dinky waits all day to hold Tiny Baby. She has no memories of Baby Boy, born when she was one. This time, at the mature age of seven, she insists on holding and seeing.

Little Old Ladies Society sews tiny clothes with tiny blanket for tiny babies. At one and a half pounds, he is important. He is loved. We hold him for hours.

We want a real funeral for a real baby. Mortician comes, asks questions about the type of service we want, then finally asks, "Are you ready for me to take him?"

Yes, of course. It's time. We can't hold him forever.

I hand Tiny Baby over to him. He gently cradles the small bundle and says, "I'll take good care of him." Such tenderness. So caring. Much peace.

Until he starts out the door with Tiny Baby. Unexpected pain wells up, screaming inside, *"No! I'm not ready! I want him back! Bring him back!"*

Pain is too heavy. Heart is breaking. Must take it to Jesus. I place Tiny Baby in loving, nail-scarred hands of Jesus.

Evening nurse says fever must be gone before I can leave. The first nurse to verbally express sympathy for baby loss, she changes sheets, walks me to the bathroom, helps me dress in dry clothes. Gentle. Not in a hurry. Tenderness and compassion in every service. A caring smile, a soft voice. I study her name tag - R.N. "Why are you doing this? Shouldn't nurse's aides handle the yucky stuff?"

She smiles. "I do whatever I can to help." She embodies the nursing moniker, "Angel of Mercy."

I melt into her kindness. *"Why wasn't she on duty this morning?"*

I ride with empty arms in my wheelchair taxi toward the exit sign. No one speaks. We drive home in a daze and go quietly to bed. Panic wakes me with a jolt at 3:00 a.m. I shout at Coach, "I cried out to God, and He didn't hear me!"

Who said that? It can't be me! Coach stares at me for a second, then goes back to sleep.

Swirl of thoughts. Once again, long-held beliefs are shaken. I always teach my kids to cry out to God if they are ever in any trouble. "God will deliver you," I tell them. Yet, I cry out to God all through labor, and never even sense His presence. Something is wrong!

I charge down a dark hallway to the living room to find God. I grab a Bible; open it at random. The book of Job. First verse I see: "I cried out to God, and He did not hear me. I stood before Him, and he did not regard me" (Job 30:20).

Next verse: "God has been cruel to me."

Shocking silence. Job feels like I do. He says my words. And God calls Job a "perfect and upright man" (Job 1:8).

I analyze. I process. I know God is everywhere, even delivery rooms, but in that horrible life-wrenching moment, He doesn't do what I want him to do. I want Him to stop the pain, stop the death, but He doesn't.

"God, what *did* You do?"

"I kept you alive." Not audible, but the message is instant, clear, and distinct in my spirit.

Mental screen replays the image of a monitor by my hospital bed. Nurse leaves Coach alone with me to wake me when it beeps. Tired Coach falls asleep. Beeping repeatedly interrupts my slumber.

"That annoying beep! What does it mean? I'm supposed to do something, but, what? What? ...Oh, Breathe!" Take a breath to make it stop. God keeps me alive. He knows my history. The Great Physician never leaves my side. He keeps watch when all others are gone. He keeps me alive.

"Because of the Lord's faithful love, we do not perish" (Lam 3:22, HCSB).

Anger

ISAAC ISN'T THE perfect name, anymore. No more laughter. Coach suggests Jeremiah – the weeping prophet. Perfect.

Funeral service at the grave site on a Sunday afternoon. Break all traditions. Something different. Two preachers and Coach speak at the service. Coach, three young brothers, Uncle, and Pops want to dig the grave themselves. *Why?* Coach says it is an honor to do this for his son - the one he thought would change the world.

No guilt this time around. I know better. It's not my fault. So....whose fault is it? I want to blame someone. But who? God? We don't ask for this pregnancy. But we embrace it when it comes. Then Someone jerks hope right out from under us. Like a cruel joke. Yes, I'm angry at God.

Angry at Coach, too. He doesn't understand. He doesn't want me to cry or snuggle for comfort. He wants to dress in camo, stuff his pockets with snacks, and sit in deer stands all day. He wants me to get over it.

Angry at everyone. Hardly any meals or flowers - not like when Baby Boy died. Don't they know a mother's love is just as strong for a tiny baby as for a full-term baby? Don't they know I'm miserable? They don't understand. I never understood before, either.

Anger grows. Pain grows. Too sick at heart to eat most days. I try to muddle through, but give in to defeat. I sit in my bedroom floor, lean on the bed and cry, "God, I need help!"

Instantly, the phone rings. Lady from the funeral home asks if I want a copy of the death certificate. I can't answer. I choke out, "It is just so hard."

Lady replies, "It *IS* hard, and *NO ONE* understands!" Her words startle and comfort. She has a grief share group. She offers to deliver the papers to me and listen to my story.

Kids are busy with Coach, so grey-haired Lady stays two hours and listens, hears my pain. She says, "When a person goes through two griefs back to back, the pain is doubled. Events pile up together."

She's right. Tears drop for Tiny Baby, then for Baby Boy five minutes later. Two deaths muddle into one tragedy, as if they happen simultaneously.

Lady says, "Let yourself grieve, or you will fall apart over something really small." Like when I cry because I get lost taking Beauty to basketball practice? She's right again.

Lady shows "grieving" folders that say anger is normal. But I don't want to be normal! I want to be Super Saint - rising above it all with rejoicing and praise! Must I settle for normal? Sigh.

Lady says, "Guilt and anger are flip-sides of the same coin: Blame." Surely, someone is to blame for this! With Baby Boy, I blame myself; with Tiny Baby, I blame God. I forget that God never promises life without pain or suffering. Bible says the *whole creation* groans in pain, waiting for our bodies to be redeemed (Rom 8:22-23). Adam's sin in the garden's dew brings pain, suffering, death to everyone. Man is *born* into trouble (Job 5:7). God doesn't choose that. Adam does. "When Adam sinned, sin entered the world. Adam's sin brought death, so death spread to everyone, for everyone sinned" (Rom 5:12 NLT). The sentence of death comes with our birth.

So, now, do I blame Adam? He blames the wife. And she blames the snake. The snake's fault! Satan, the snake, comes to steal, kill, and destroy (Jn 10:10). Can't blame God for that. God comes to bring life. He lets Adam choose because He doesn't want robots. Adam chooses death, and the world groans. Waiting…

Paul the Apostle knows all about suffering. He writes: "For I reckon that the sufferings of this present time are not worthy to be compared with the glory which shall be revealed in us" (Rom 8:18). This slice of mortal time is full of misery. But the memory of this suffering and death will totally disappear when held next to the indescribable glory that is to come.

Step back to see the Bigger picture. Immortality. Hope. This all makes sense, rings true, but the longing remains. Hope says I'll see him again, but the Heart wants him now.

Purpose

GOD SENDS ANOTHER listener to help me interpret emotions. I feel like a child; angry that my toy is taken away. Life doesn't do what I want it to do. Bold Friend asks, "But, what do we deserve?"

"Nothing."

If we all got what we deserve, we would all be dead. We would possess nothing. "It is by his mercies we are not consumed" (Lam 3:22).

Counselors say anger is a cover for vulnerability, fear, or pain. My anger is a feeble cover for pain. Too much pain! I ask Jesus to carry the pain for me. Not just once; many times. What's the problem? I wrestle with questions. The mind stretches to understand, but it can't. If I want to release the pain to Jesus, I also have to surrender the questions that torment. Once again, I must give up my right to know what God is doing. Trust Him. God yearns for me to trust Him. Trust Him to work it for my good. Satan may have intended it for evil, but God intended it for good (Gen 50:20).

My Bible says, "Cast all your anxiety on him, because he cares for you" (1 Pet 5:7, NRSV).

When I am finally ready to cast all unanswered questions on Jesus, the pain and anger go, too.

But one thought lingers. Tiny Baby was supposed to have some great purpose – Coach was sure of it. I believed him. Was he wrong?

Lanky One thinks deep, "Mom, we were so sad that our Tiny Baby died, but there are aborted babies the same size as ours, and no one is sad for them." He connects the dots. He knows even a Tiny Baby is still a person, a brother, a friend. He grieves for all small babies. It hurts.

Tiny Baby still has a purpose; can still be used by God for His Kingdom. His brief time on this planet can point the way to life. "Before I formed you in the womb I knew you; before you were born I sanctified you" (Jer 1:5, NKJV).

In my pain, someone throws a lifeline, a quote by Ugo Bassi (1848):

"Measure thy life by loss and not by gain,
not by the wine drunk, but by the wine poured forth.
For love's strength stands in love's sacrifice,
and he that suffers most has most to give."

Surprises

FIVE MONTHS LATER, who cares what people think? No one is stealing my joy! Surrender reputation. Let them think what they want. Tell everyone I'm expecting, again!

Doctors all warn against this pregnancy. It's foolish, they say. Not wise. But wisdom is not the issue here. The issue is trust and obedience. I made a commitment to God: He can have my body. I can't go back on that. Easier to trust God than to worry what will happen next. Fear is conquered by faith.

I announce the "blessed event" as a prayer request at Church Ladies Meeting. Crickets. Finally, Bold Lady, never at a loss for words, ventures, "I don't know what to say."

All quiet, I suddenly have the floor. I share the Courageous story of Joseph Tson:

Born in communist Romania, Joseph is allowed to attend college in America. He tells everyone he plans to return to his home country as a missionary after graduation. All voices are negative. "Don't do it! You'll be arrested! You'll be beaten! What chance do you have for success?"

Joseph, never even considering the potential for success, thinks only of obedience to God's voice. But now, in his dorm room, these new concerns turn into prayers: "Lord, what chance do I have of success?"

The Holy Spirit answers Joseph with a mental image of wolves surrounding a sheep (Mat 10:16). "What chance does the sheep have of survival, let alone converting the wolves?"

None, of course. But Joseph anguishes over the question in his heart: "Why do you allow this scenario for your servants?"

God answers, "The blood of faithful martyrs has always planted the seeds of the church."

"So," I explain to speechless ladies, "The concern for us sheep should not be 'success' or even 'survival,' but instead, 'obedience' and 'trust.' If God calls us, it is not our place to analyze the probability of success. This pregnancy may not be successful, but my job is to obey. God has a plan, and I am just following it."

Bold Lady sighs in resignation, not fully understanding. "Well… we're behind you, honey. We'll be praying."

New Faces

THIS TIME: NEW hospital, new doctor, one hour away from home. I choose a fatherly sort of doctor who's been catching babies for years. Very conservative, he lets me do whatever I want with birth plan.

This time: visit nutritionist to be as healthy as possible for this pregnancy. I have varicose veins, racing heart, insomnia, very dry skin, hair and mouth, and I'm 41. He says I'm not digesting my food. Too nervous? He says eat more often, drink carrot juice, and take handful of supplements, along with digestive enzymes. Keep food by the bed and eat when I awake during the night. I like this guy.

This time: Eight-year-old Pinky Dinky goes with me to ultrasound appointment. She wants a girl. I remember her two-day crying spell when she discovered Tiny Baby's gender. She can go on one condition: no crying if it's a boy.

In route to the clinic, I remind her: have self-control if this baby is a boy. In the waiting room, I re-enforce gratefulness no matter what gender God gives us. She agrees.

Breathless Pinky Dinky and I wait while friendly technician clicks thousands of pictures. Then, finally, she announces, "O.K. Let's see if you are going to get a little brother or a little sister."

Desperate Trust

Drumroll, please...

Pinky Dinky quickly slides off her chair and stands by me to see better; anxious. I turn to small, intent face, and silently mouth, "Don't cry."

She nods, solemn, with eyes glued to the screen. This is serious.

Long seconds later, technician proclaims, "Looks like a sister!"

Pinky Dinky cheers, and I break into body-shaking sobs! Hormonal explosion? Can't stop *bawling*. Tech hands me a towel and coos, "Looks like you wanted a girl, too!"

I can't explain it. Maybe relief that this new baby looks healthy? Maybe thinking a different gender will have a different outcome? Maybe sharing happiness with Pinky Dinky? Whatever the reason, Pink can't understand why she is banned from crying, but Mom is allowed to blubber like a baby!

Labor Room Madness

Eight months along, and baby is LARGE, so one more ultrasound. Seven and a half pound baby with one long month to go. We agree: induce labor at thirty-eight weeks to keep Little Mama from popping. That puts Baby Girl's birth in the bullseye on the calendar with all the other January birthdays, each exactly one week apart. Very important to an organizer.

Up at 3:00 a.m.; hospital by 5:00 a.m. Why do doctors do things so early? Pitocin IV needle brings memories of Tiny Baby flooding over anxious mind. It has only been 14 months. Sweet nurse cries with me as I recount my story. There's a sadness here. Still grieving. Baby Girl might die, too. Nothing is certain.

Nurses mention video restrictions. I always wonder who would want a video of idiotic screaming and naked bottoms. They explain: the patients with epidurals are the ones taking videos. Well, that makes more sense.

Old Trusty is doula this time. I post her by phone of slow progress. Contractions were steady at first, but now they stop.

"Is someone in the room making you nervous, inhibited?" she ponders.

"Contractions stopped when the preacher came in." Funny.

Trusty explodes, "You can't labor with a preacher in the room! Throw him out!"

Don't want to be rude. Call the nurse, pretend to need the restroom. She says, "Just unplug everything and go by yourself." Great.

Preacher hears intercom instructions and runs for the door. We pass out his coat and bid him adieu. Poor man dawdles for twenty hours in waiting room watching TV with Grandparents.

Pitocin drips eight lethargic hours and no dilation. Doc changes methods to the same medication used with Tiny Baby. Now, we're getting somewhere, but not fast enough to have Baby Girl on the "right day." Nurse looks at the clock. "Probably not tonight."

I don't care anymore. Just get this over. I give up plans for four birthdays in a row on the calendar. That's tough when you're OCD. Another surrender.

Kids call throughout labor, enjoying their big day of freedom. No parent at home means marathon eating, videos, and computer games. Life is good. Lanky One reminds me of his baby name picks: Banana Chip or Sweet Potato. I promise they are on the list. Silly guy is always proposing name themes for his future family – he will name them all after vegetables, cars, letters of the alphabet, etc. We caution him his future wife may have an opinion about that.

Coach tapes pictures of kids on T.V. screen. I pray for them, one by one, through contractions. Helps me focus. Much better than "Blow!"

Trusty and Doc are old friends. He is comfortable with her knowledge, not threatened by her suggestions. Trusty does much of the coaching, since Coach fixates on the contraction monitor bar graph. Mesmerizing.

When I get loud, Coach shifts his gaze, more observing than coaching. He's happy to take a back seat to Trusty. Roomful of stray nurses show up to view the birth. Looking back, I don't blame them. I would, too. Births are magical, hopeful, emotional. Fun for everyone but me. I still worry about people seeing me. Still modest after all these years.

Manic pushing pays off, and baby Chub arrives before the midnight bell. Bingo! Four birthdays in a row!

Screaming red bundle doesn't quiet down until I speak to her, personally. Black eyes lock with mine and she studies, stops crying. Short cord won't let us nurse (again), so Chub and I stare at each other. Intense. We heart-to-heart until Doc is ready to cut her loose.

"Is this really my baby? What am I doing with a baby?" Surreal moment never felt before or since. The brain can't comprehend, but the heart melts with her gaze.

So thankful we didn't "throw in the towel" years ago, like all suggested. So grateful for the commitment to an All-Knowing God to let Him control my life and my body. So indebted to the Holy Spirit for shoving truth in front of lies.

Desperate trust in God's *sovereignty* gives peace when there are no real options. Savage trust in God's *goodness* keeps one shoulder off the mat when fear tries to pin me. Fierce trust in God's *power* hangs on tight when the Enemy threatens to defeat me.

Yes, we *wrestle* (Eph 6:12). Yes, we *fight* (2 Tim 4:7). Trusting God is not a cake-walk.

We *press hard* for the crown (Phil 3:14). But there *IS* a crown. *Land of Rest* is on the other side, not here.

Free Will gives us choices to avoid life's potential pain, but Surrender allows for the joy and amazement of the Unexpected.

The Unplanned.

The Mysteries.

The Miracles.

God.

Afterward

SHERI EASTER (EYES Wide Open. 2012) pens a song I wish I had written myself. A fitting tribute to survivors.

<u>I Know How It Feels To Survive</u>
    Been afraid, been confused,
    Doubted everything I thought that I knew,
    But I've felt peace, and I've been loved,
    Got back on my feet thanking God above.

    'Cause I know how it feels to walk out of a valley,
    How it feels to breathe the air that gives me life,
    I know the silence that comes with trusting and believing,
    And the darkness when the shadows hide the light;
    I know how it feels to survive.

    Been alone, felt betrayed,
    Didn't know if I could stand another day;
    But I've found joy, and I have faith,
    I know the strength that gets me through one more day;

'Cause I know how it feels to walk out of a valley,
How it feels to breathe the air that gives me life,
I know the silence that comes with trusting and believing,
And the darkness when the shadows hide the light;
I know how it feels to survive.

Now I live with eyes wide open,
And my heart is filled with gratitude,
I know everything I have is only borrowed,
And by the grace of God I know I'll make it through.

'Cause I know how it feels to walk out of a valley,
How it feels to breathe the air that gives me life,
I know the silence that comes with trusting and believing,
And the darkness when the shadows hide the light;
I know how it feels to survive.

References

Thompson, Phyllis. *Hudson Taylor: God's Venturer.* Chicago, IL: Moody Press.

Goodman, Rusty. (1990). Standing in the Presence of the King. *The Reunion.*

Hayford, Jack W.. (1990). *I'll Hold You in Heaven: Healing and Hope for the Parent who has Lost a Child.* Ventura, CA: Regal Books.

George, Elizabeth. (1994). *Loving God with all Your Mind.* Eugene, OR: Harvest House Publishers.

Ministries:

Transformation Prayer Ministry has helped us, beyond any other form of counseling, to replace lies with truth. Unfortunately, we discovered it many years past the traumatic event.

Immanuel Interventions is a similar counseling ministry which focuses on bringing a sense of peace to painful memories.

WellspringMinistries (Art Matthias) and *Be In Health* (Henry Wright) both offer week-long soul-searching conferences which result in healing on many levels.

We cannot, of course, give a blanket endorsement to any ministry which is staffed by fallible humans, but there are some very useful components in each of these. We are still in process. Still chipping away at the lies that were implanted in the wounds.

Made in the USA
Middletown, DE
13 August 2022